Seneca Ray Stoddard

Ticonderoga, past and present

A Companion to Lake George

Seneca Ray Stoddard

Ticonderoga, past and present
A Companion to Lake George

ISBN/EAN: 9783741103100

Manufactured in Europe, USA, Canada, Australia, Japa

Cover: Foto ©ninafisch / pixelio.de

Manufactured and distributed by brebook publishing software
(www.brebook.com)

Seneca Ray Stoddard

Ticonderoga, past and present

TICON·DEROGA:

PAST AND PRESENT.

"MIXED."

A COMPANION TO "LAKE GEORGE, ILLUSTRATED."

BEING A HISTORY OF TICONDEROGA — ILLUSTRATED WITH ETCH-
INGS, AND CONTAINING A MAP OF THE RUINS OF TO-DAY.

BY

S. R. STODDARD.

ALBANY:

WEED, PARSONS AND COMPANY, PRINTERS.

1873.

WEED, PARSONS & CO.,
PRINTERS AND STEREOTYPERS,
ALBANY, N. Y.

TABLE OF CONTENTS.

67903

TICONDEROGA.

OVERLAND.

ANDERERS still, we have threaded the silvery pathway of the Horican, and are drifting idly toward the gray old ruins of the forest stronghold, venerable in its departed grandeur, crowned with the wild legends and historical associations that cluster around its crumbling battlements and telling its story of loves and hates, of hopes and fears, of the glittering pomps of warfare, of booming cannon and the rolling drum, of glad pæans of victory, the solemn dirge, of death. Of earthly plans, of ambitions wild, of the arrogant assumption of puny man, and the love of forgiving Nature, who tenderly covers over the scars and hides the ruined hopes under a mantle of living green.

The trip overland from Lake George to Lake Champlain cannot, strictly speaking, be called a green spot in the memory, for my recollection of the place is that it almost always rains, or has just been doing so, in which case the *spots* are a decided

clay color; but they who fail to take it in are, to
say the least, unfortunate, and miss one of the finest
features of a trip to Ticonderoga, for there are more
recollections piled into the hour occupied in crossing than days spent elsewhere.

Five great box-like stages, one baggage wagon,
twenty-two horses and six drivers waited for us at
the foot of Lake George, as the little steamer came
to rest against the dock, and we passed out over
the plank to the clay-bespattered platform, where
stood the driver-in-chief, with always a pleasant
word or a happy retort at his tongue's end, and a
fund of information at the disposal of any who might
take the trouble to ask for it; a genial, obliging,
gentlemanly man; the joy of seekers after knowledge; the terror of those who know too much, and
the admiration of unprotected females, who, blessed
with a multitude of years and bundles, have been
robbed and execrated everywhere else in consequence thereof; one who transports his passengers
with safety and wit, and actually seems to think
them possessed of privileges which a stage driver
is bound to respect.   In short, it is " Baldwin," and
that tells it all, for every body knows him.

" Mr. Baldwin, I presume," said a young man,
with a smart air, approaching the veteran.

"At your service, sir."

" My name is Smith."

"Ah! Your fame has preceded you, sir; you are spoken of at some length in the city directory. Hope you are feeling well."

"Quite so, thank you. May I venture to inquire how the animals are getting along?"

"Certainly; quite naturally. They are doing *very* well, considering the depth of the mud. I have been very fortunate so far, sir; never have lost an animal yet, although they often get in out of sight, in which case we take their bearings, and raise them at our leisure."

"I do not refer to your *horses*," said the young man, with a quizzical look at the great, red stage, and coming to the point at once: "But do you know, sir, that you and your caravan remind me of Barnum with his cages of wonderful wild animals."

"Can't see the least resemblance, my dear sir," said Baldwin; "for Barnum carries *his* animals inside, while *mine* usually ride on top. Climb up, if you please."

After we were fairly under way a gentleman asked Mr. Baldwin if he was any relation to the Baldwin *apple*.

"Yes, sir: we are first cousins."

"Ah! I am delighted to know it. I'm Mr. Pippin."

"Proud to make your acquaintance, sir," said the Baldwin; "happy to know that we both belong to the same great family; but I have noticed, I am sorry to say, that pippins, while outwardly fair to behold, are usually rotten at the core."

Pippin was dried apples for the rest of the journey.

Immediately after the close of the late unpleasantness at the south the country was full of shoulder-straps and bullion, and almost every little hamlet boasted its General — a Brigadier at least. One day, at Ticonderoga, one of these titled gentlemen might have been, and *was*, seen taking possession of a top seat on one of Baldwin's stages, considerably elevated, spiritually as well as bodily, and evidently anxious to match his wit against that of the noted joker. He opened the engagement by inquiring if Phil Sheridan had not passed that way in his recent trip through the country, and was told that he had.

" Well," said he, " how was the General at the time? he's rather given to the demi, isn't he?"

"Do you mean demi-*john?*"

" Yes!"

" Well, I don't know, but he may be," said Mr. Baldwin, "its a common affliction among my military passengers."

" Come, come!" said the General, producing a pocket-flask, and offering it, evidently feeling that his opponent's remarks were rather pointed, "take a drink, and let's call it square."

"No, sir!" said he, "I do not use the stuff: I propose to live without it, and die with my wits about me."

"Very good, if a man can't stand it, he'd better not try. *You* are a good man; a moral man; and a re-*markably* good-looking man, I must confess; but, say, how is it, does it take a re-*markably* good-looking man to make a stage-driver?"

"Yes, *sir!*" said the remarkably good-looking man, evidently on his mettle, "It takes a *man* for a stage-driver, but any thing under heaven will do for a General, now-a-days!"

We mount to the top of the hill, where we must bid adieu to the silvery waters, and a lovely scene of sloping hillside, valley and mountain, opens up before us. Then down the road we go to the corner, where, turning to cross the bridge, above the falls, we pause a moment and look around.

Here the waters of the lake that have moved sluggishly along between their low banks begin to ripple and gurgle as if they heard the music, and were hurrying gleefully onward to join in the glad anthem of the sounding waters below, and passing under the bridge, rest a moment in their course, then, flashing and foaming, plunge downward, in a succession of leaps, until they rest under the cloud of spray at the bottom. Now, singing through the meadows, dancing over the stones, sweeping around to the right, they go, ever hurrying, never resting, until they gather for their final leap over the outcropping ledges at the lower falls that separates the mass of water into threads of shining silver and myriads of glittering pearls.

Here is one of the best mill privileges in the world, furnished with a uniform supply of water, through drouth or flood, from the never failing reservoir above, making a descent of over two hundred feet in going a little more than a mile, while large vessels can be brought up to the very foot of the lower falls, and laid against the mills from which to receive their cargoes.

At one time quite a village existed here, rejoicing in the name of Alexandria, but the land was owned by an Englishman, who refused to sell without exacting onerous terms, such as a reservation of all ores, minerals, etc., to himself and heirs for all time to come, which has kept it comparatively unoccupied. Once, a good many years ago, men came to look at the falls, with intent to build, but, not considering the title good, they went to Lowell and commenced the erection of these immense factories which have made the place what it is; and thus Ticonderoga lost its chance of ranking among cities where Lowell does to-day. Within a year

or two, however, a company from that city has
erected a cotton factory at the foot of the falls,
which will give employment to nearly two hundred
operatives, which state of affairs causes great joy
in the breasts of the young men thereabout, and
Alexandria is looking up once more.

Toward the north, down where the waters of the
lake, circling around, are joined by those of Trout
Brook from the valley on the west, the gallant Lord
Howe — the life and actual leader of Abercrombie's
unfortunate expedition of 1758 — was killed.   He
is described as having been the very personification
of boldness and enterprise; having but few equals
physically, and perfectly at home whether in the
halls of royalty or among the sturdy colonists —
the life of every movement with which he was con-
nected — and seeing, not the dress or grade, social
or military, but the man, whether robed in royal
purple or clothed in homespun.   He had conceived
a great liking for Rogers, admired him for his
daring and skill as a woodsman, and often joined
him on his expeditions to master the mysteries
of bush fighting, and match himself against the
wily red men in their native forests.

A letter written by one who accompanied the
expedition states that Lord Howe was with Putnam, at the head of the rangers, pressing through
the thick forests toward Ticonderoga, when they

came suddenly upon a detachment of 300 French, who, in attempting to retreat to the fort, had lost their way.

"Keep back, my lord," said Putnam, as they advanced toward the enemy; "you are the idol and soul of the army, while *my* life is worth but little."

"Putnam," was Howe's answer, "your life is as dear to you as mine is to me. I am determined to go.'

At the first fire Lord Howe fell, and the whole English army was thrown into confusion, the regulars pressing back on those behind in a way that, for a time, threatened a complete rout. The rangers, taking refuge behind trees, fought on after the Indian fashion, until the main body rallied and returned to the charge, this time sweeping the French before them with great slaughter, killing one-third of their number and taking about one hundred and fifty prisoners.

The death of Howe seemed to paralyze the men for a time, who, confused and disheartened by their loss, returned to the landing or bivouacked on the field until the next day, when they advanced upon the French lines.

Crossing the bridge we proceed on our way, and, soon turning again toward the north, commence descending the long hill that leads down to the village of Ticonderoga.

Many admire the surrounding country, but no one goes into ecstacies over the roads. We are not, apparently, educated up to it; but if the lamented Captain Jack could come here when the clay has hardened into rock, and gaze down into the yawning depths of the caverncus ruts, his bones would leap for joy, thinking that they were once more among the lava beds of the Modoc country. Then, when it has been raining, and the rock softens, *all* idols have feet of clay, and it does not require such a wonderful stretch of faith to believe that you are actually made of the dust of the earth, for there is indisputable proof all over you.

> Clay to the right of them ;
> Clay to the left of them ;
> Front, back and top of 'em.
> Slippery and squashy.

Sticky doesn't half express the agony — it meets you half way every time ; it works steadily up your legs ; it clings to your boots, building out at the sides, piling up and rolling over on top, in front, behind — *every* way. Occasionally, when you are exerting yourself to lift a foot, it will break off in great masses so unexpectedly that you nearly go over on the other side ; then load up again, and increasing in size and weight until in general appearance and style of handling (if a person may be properly said to handle his

2

feet) they resemble those of the agile elephant, and
you cease to wonder that flies walk fearlessly on
the ceiling, if the suction on their pedal extremities
is any thing like that of yours in Ticonderoga clay.
Great masses revolve ponderously over on the
wheels; the coaches are painted, striped and var-
nished with it, the drivers are covered, and the
horses look like clay models of that noble beast.

The stages halted in a cluster when part way
down the hill, and looking around to see the cause
of the stoppage we beheld a Websterian form
(some suggested that it was more Clay than Web-
ster — from the knees down) mounted on a ros-
tral pile of stones, and thus the orator spake :

"Ladies and gentlemen, you will see, if you
please, on your left, a great natural curiosity — an
oak and an elm growing from one stump; you can
see by the bark and by the leaves that there is no
mistake about it; it is truly a g-r-e-a-t n-a-t-u-r-a-l
c-u-r-i-o-s-i-t-y ; and what God has joined together
let not man put asunder; *drive* on your horses."

"*Hold* on !" shouted a confident young blood, who
saw a chance of turning the laugh on the renowned
joker.

"Woa! woa! what's up?"

With a majestic wave of the hand, in imitation
of the speaker who had preceded him, he said :

"You will behold, if you please, on the *right*,

another g-r-e-a-t n-a-t-u-r-a-l c-u-r-i-o-s-i-t-y; a juvenile specimen of the bovine race—"

" Young man," said Baldwin, sternly "that's a *calf*. No great curiosity to any one who has seen you. Drive on, George."

This curious tree spoken of has a smooth, round body, which, a little above the surface, separates into two distinct species, as stated by Mr. Baldwin, who, on being asked how he accounted for the phenomenon, allowed that it was " because it grew on good union soil."

" Ruins! ruins! Let us roam," said a gentleman who seemed to be afflicted with a defective vision and a poetic temperament. " Fit emblem of the poor, weak mortals who here strove for fame, and now forgotten lie in unknown graves; while Time, the great leveler, passes, and the mighty walls of Ticonderoga crumble away into the dust;—and, I say, driver, can you show us the underground passage that we hear so much talk about?"

" *Yes*, sir, when we get there; I should be very happy. This is not the *ruins*, however, but the thriving little village of Ticonderoga. A little dirty, I must admit, owing to the conditions of the roads, but a pretty little village, indeed, when it gets washed up."

The village has a thrifty look; contains about 1,500 inhabitants, three or four churches, schools, an academy, woolen factory — noted for producing a remarkably good quality of cloth — two hotels, several stores, black lead mill, etc.; soil very productive and roads — characteristic.

We pass through the village, across the bridge, turn toward the right, descend a steep little pitch to the flat below, and circling around to the other side climb the hill, halting at intervals that the panting horses may get breath for a fresh pull at the heavy stages.

Glancing backward we see the lovely little village; its white houses and church spires gleaming through the dark green foliage of oaks, shut in by mountains that come down round about on every side; the divided falls flashing and foaming white, with a foreground of waving grasses and lily-pads; while through the reedy flat comes the stream, winding gently onward to where it mingles with the waters of Champlain, under the gray walls of Ticonderoga.

Arriving at the top of the hill we find a broad plateau, along which, in a south-easterly direction, we go, and entering a field through a gate, which is opened by a muddy little boy, are upon the bloody battle ground in front of the old French lines.

ABERCROMBIE'S DEFEAT.

LITTLE after noon, on the 8th of July, 1758, the order was given to advance, and the English army swept forward "into the jaws of death" to attack the French, who were securely entrenched behind high breastworks; while extending out in front for a hundred yards oak trees had been felled, and lay with the branches sharpened, and pointing outward. Up to this the English marched, and endeavored to force their way, while a steady fire from the enemy cut lanes and alleys through their columns, and swept them away like leaves before the whirlwind.

Three times did the Scotch Highlanders cut their way to the very summit of the ramparts, and while some, toppling over, pierced with many wounds, fell fighting to the last, the rest borne back by the furious storm of iron which flew from that line of fire, retreated sullenly to re-form for another advance.

For four hours, under the hot July sun, this unequal contest lasted, the English columns advancing like waves of the ocean, to dash in

impotent fury upon that terrific shore of death,
and, breaking, recede in rivulets of blood.   The
recall sounded at last, and they retreated in dis-
order — frightened when no man pursueth — to
their boats at Lake George, where they re-em-
barked, and returned to Fort William Henry without bringing a cannon to bear on the enemy.

Abercrombie reported 588 killed and missing,
and 1,356 wounded.   Of this number the Forty-
second Highlanders alone lost, killed and wounded,
over 600, including all but two of its officers.
The loss would have been much greater if there
had been a force of Indians for Montcalm to set
after the fugitives ; but, luckily, there were but
sixteen in the fort at the time.   The French force
engaged was 3,458 ; loss, 271 wounded ; 197 killed
and missing.

At its close Montcalm, who had stood with his
coat off throughout the entire engagement, direct-
ing the movements of his men, made the proud
boast that, with a half dozen guns and two mortars,
he could take Carillon without the loss of a man,
thinking, probably, of Mount Defiance ; but Abercrombie did not seem to think of that, although he
had that very day sent an engineer to reconnoitre,
and Gen. Johnson, with 600 Indians, occupied, and
from its summit were silent spectators of the scene
below.

When Abercrombie ordered the advance, he took up his position at the saw-mills, a mile in the rear (a post of great danger in case the roof should happen to fall in), where he valiantly remained until a retreat was decided upon, when, with unparalleled bravery, he gallantly lead the advance toward home.

The muddy little ˙ oy who opened the gate for us was not there at that time. It is to be deeply regretted that such was the case; for, if he *had* been, and firmly refused to allow them to enter without a permit from the Pell heirs, thereby compelling the brilliant General to take some other road to reach the battle-ground, we would not now be called upon to chronicle the sad event; but the M. L. B. was not there. There were no reliable guide-books out at the time, and as Baldwin utterly refused to carry the army over for a single cent less than the regular fare, they waded; and the result should be a warning to any who are base enough to insinuate that the *hills* are not the only steep things on the route.

We cross the "old French lines," full of angles, fronted by a deep ditch, and extending through the woods to the water on either side, past two or three redouts, and, where the cars shoot through the hill beneath us, come in sight of the ruins, a quarter of a mile distant.

What memories cluster around the gray old promontory? What a history is thine, oh, crumbling Ticonderoga? Enough for another chapter! So, let us hasten to the hotel, down among the locusts, where a good dinner is awaiting, after which we can moralize, and paw among the ruins to our heart's content; but, stop! Behold a towering form standing, proudly erect, on that pile of stones, and snuffing in inspiration by the quart! Baldwin is himself once more! and the very heavens seem to stoop down to listen to his farewell flights of fancy. How magnificently he spreads his wings, and soars away from the sorrowful past into the glorious future, mounting away up, up, among the glittering constellation of stars — and stripes, one and inseparable — of America's coming greatness — at, including the ride, seventy-five cents per head.

And right here let us pause in our gayety to drop a silent tear for one whose life has been overshadowed by a great earthly affliction. Many anecdotes are told illustrative of his readiness to reply. The only instance on record where he failed was on the occasion of General Sherman's passage through the lake in 1871. He had entertained the company with his usual historical flights of fancy along the road, and was introduced to the General, by Captain Babbitt as "Captain Baldwin."

As the boat moved away, he proposed three
cheers for the " Hero of Atlanta!" General Sherman, not to be outdone, stepped out from the company, and said:

"Captain Baldwin! I promote you to Colonel
for meritorious conduct on the old battle-ground."

The great stage man was not prepared for *that*.
The unexpected honor was too much for him, and,
for the first time in his life (when talking with a
man), he failed to get in the last word. The horrid
conviction of the fact forced itself upon him when
too late, and he stood, gazing helplessly at the
departing boat, until his faithful drivers, gathering
near, asked, in tones of sweet sympathy, whether
he intended to ride back or wade. Then they
gently led the stricken man to the waiting stages,
and bore him back to his home. Tenderly they
put him in his little bed; lovingly they watched
over him, while pitying neighbors gathered tear-
fully around the sufferer, whose spirit, for many,
many days, seemed just hovering between this
world and Ticonderoga; then he was snatched
away from the fell destroyer, and once more
appeared in the old, familiar places; but, alas! he
went forth a changed man. He had learned the
lesson of life; and since that fearful day has ceased
to be surprised at any thing. Even when he offered
President Grant a handful of cigars, and he took

but one, the shock was but momentary, and he soon
recovered from its effects. Alas! No more shall
we hear his ringing shout of joy! but the sad,
sweet smile, that illumines his face, grows more
spirituel as the years drag slowly by.   Ah!

"Few know how great a thing it is to suffer, and be strong!"

Soon, very soon, will he be done with his earthly
wanderings, and his spirit looks forward with a joy
that few can know to the happy moment when,
bidding adieu to the well-remembered scenes of
his pilgrimage here below, he will brush the clay
from off his garments, and, with a new song in his
mouth and a punch in his hand, soar away over
the Lake George and Ticonderoga Railroad, a
blissful, free conductor.

DISCOVERIES.

A RETROSPECT.

S the distance to a certain star is ascertained by the science of triangulation — finding its relative position in the heavens as viewed from different places in the earth's orbit, so must we go back a little way and note a few important points in history to enable us understandingly to place in time the history of this particular locality.

In the year one Adam and Eve discovered the garden of Eden and began business.

A few hundred years later Noah built an ark-itectural craft, and, combining business with pleasure, went on a voyage of discovery, being the first man

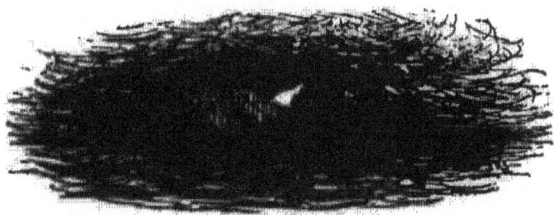

of whom we have any record as traveling with a menagerie. He was not very well patronized, however, on account of the Black Croo¹:, which was having an unprecedented run at that time; and although he advertised it extensively for a hundred and twenty years, he only got together an audience of seven beside himself, and all deadheads at that. So one time, when he accidentally got aground, he was discouraged (Barnum wouldn't have been, but he was), gave up the show business, settled on Mount Ararat, and went into the liquor trade.

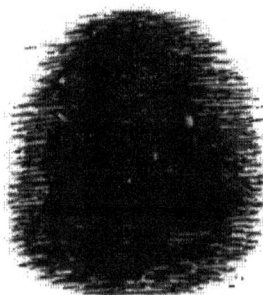

The next discovery (let us say it reverently, for the bright angels assisted, and beside it all others are as naught) was made by the wise men of the east, who found in a manger a little baby form, within which trembled the sweet spirit of the Savior of mankind.

Then a thousand years went by, and, tradition says, the northmen came to the shores of the western continent, and sailing as far south as Rhode Island attempted to settle there; then they drifted back again, and the country was as though it had never been seen.

In 1492 America was discovered some more by C. Columbus, who attained to considerable local notoriety thereby. All young men should copy after this great and good man — now, alas, deceased — and discover new countries.

It is true, all do not possess the advantages which he did, and cannot expect to do as well; but all can *try*. It is a subject to which the author has given considerable, deep, exhaustive study, and, while he venerates the old chap hugely for what he did, justice to another compels him to say that Chris. has been greatly over-honored, and that the actual discoverer of America was his mother-in-law. Not that she really saw it *with her own eyes,*

but history positively states that she "gave him the privilege of examining the charts and journals of her deceased husband," which led to the glorious results above mentioned, and for which she should have the credit. This point seems to have escaped the notice of all other historians. To a reflecting mind it affords food for serious contemplation, conveying, as it does, a great, double-barreled lesson; for, while it should induce all young ladies to aim at the honorable distinction of becoming what she was — viewing from a distance, which always lends enchantment to the view (of mothers-in-law) — it should teach us the lesson of greater toleration toward that interesting class.

3

In 1497 John Cabot saw Labrador or the island of " New-found-land."

In 1524 Verrazani explored the Atlantic coast from Delaware to New Foundland, and gave it the name of "New France."

In 1534 James Cartier entered the mouth of the St. Lawrence, and the following year sailed up the river to a large Indian settlement, called " Hochelaga;" but the hotel accommodations being no better, if as good as at present, he returned to France, naming the place Mount Royal — now Montreal.

In 1607 the first permanent English settlement on the new continent was commenced, the original and only true John Smith assisting, and it was called Jamestown. Smith, who seems to have been quite a tourist in his day, and given to wandering about making discoveries, had, on one of his excursions, a little misunderstanding with a wealthy native land-owner, named Powhattan. Mr. P., being endowed with a large heart and very liberal ideas, and thinking to settle the difficulty in the easiest manner possible, at the same time disseminating knowledge by scattering said Smith's well-stored brains, had him placed in the position best adapted to the satisfactory accomplishment of the same. At this very interesting juncture, his daughter, the youthful Pocahontas, cast an implor-

ing look on her father and her protecting form on
Smith. The old gentleman was touched, and con-

sented to forego his little joke to please the fair
girl, who had but just made her *debut*. Smith returned to his home, since which time every body
has been naming their children after him as a protection against Indians. Pocahontas ought to have
married him to make the romance complete, but
she did not. She became the wife of an English
gentleman, and, under that severe affliction, joined
the church, taking the name of Rebecca. Her
descendants are now found among the F. F. V.'s.

December 21, 1620, the pilgrims were discovered
sitting on Plymouth Rock, apparently lost. Winter,
which, in that favored locality, commences on the
first of August and continues until the latter part
of July, had fairly set in, and the rock was very
cold; so they got down and skirmished around for
something to eat. Luckily they found a quantity
of corn, which Providence, assisted by some of the

natives, had concealed in the sand near by, and
which enabled them to worry through   (As a

proof of Darwinianism, it may be well to state
here that they came from the May*flower*, which is
going further back than the monkey even, and out-
Darwins Darwin himself.)   They were so exces-
sively liberal-minded as to insist on every body else
being liberal, also, which occasioned a misunderstanding with one Roger Williams, who promul-
gated the pernicious doctrine that the "civil power
had no right to control the religious opinions of
men." This was too much bigotry for them to
swallow, and they very properly invited him to go.
He accepted the invitation, and fenced in a little
farm further south, which (Rodge was a plain man,
and easily satisfied) has since been known as Rhode
Island.

Eleven years before the pilgrims landed, Henry
Hudson, an English captain of a Dutch junk
called the "Semi-luna," discovered and ascended

the river that now bears his name; whereupon England laid claim to the country because of his being an Englishman, and the Dutch on the strength of the ship in which he sailed. Between the two it grew to be an English colony, with Dutch inhabitants, who gave its largest town the name of *New Amsterdam;* afterward changed to New York. It still stands.

The same year a representative of the French nation, Champlain, accompanying a war party of Hurons and Algonquins against the Iroquois, sailed south on the lake which he named after himself, then called by a jaw-breaking Indian title, which, interpreted, means "the lake that is the gate of the country." We copy his graphic account of the first battle that occurred near this place in which Europeans took a hand:

" I left the rapids of the river of the Iroquois on the 2d of July, 1609. * * * On coming within two or three days' journey of the enemy's quarters, we traveled only by night and rested by day. * * *

"At nightfall we embarked in our canoes to continue our journey, and, as we advanced very softly and noiselessly, we encountered a war party of Iroquois on the 29th of the month, about ten o'clock at night, at the point of a cape which puts into the lake on the west side. They and we began to shout,

each seizing his arms. We withdrew toward the
water, and the Iroquois repaired on shore and
arranged all their canoes, the one beside the other,
and began to hew down trees, with villainous axes,
which they sometimes got in war, and others of
stone, and fortified themselves very securely.

"Our party, likewise, kept their canoes arranged
the one alongside the other, tied to poles so as not
to run adrift, in order to fight all together, should
need be. We were on the water, about an arrow-
shot from their barricades. When they were armed
and in order, they sent two canoes from the fleet to
know if their enemies wished to fight; who
answered that they 'desired nothing else,' but that
just then there was not much light, and we must
wait for day to distinguish each other, and that they
would give us battle at sunrise. This was agreed
to by our party. Meanwhile the whole night was
spent in dancing and singing, as well on one side as
on the other, mingled with an infinitude of insults
and other taunts, such as the little courage they
had, how powerless their resistance against their
arms, and that when day would break, they should
experience this to their ruin. Ours, likewise, did
not fail in repartee ; telling them they should wit-
ness the effects of arms they had never seen before,
and a multitude of other speeches as is usual at a
siege of a town. After the one and the other had

sung, danced and parliamented enough, day broke.
My companions and I were always concealed, for
fear the enemy should see us, preparing our arms the
best we could, being, however, separated, each in
one of the canoes.   After being equipped with light
armor, we took each an arquebus and went ashore.
I saw the enemies leave their barricade; they were
about 200 men, of strong and robust appearance,
who were coming slowly toward us, with a gravity
and assurance which greatly pleased me, led on by
three chiefs.   Ours were marching in similar order,
and told me that those who bore three lofty plumes
were the chiefs, and that there were but these three,
and they were to be recognized by those plumes
which were considerably larger than those of their
companions and that I must do all I could to kill
them.   I promised to do what I could, and that I
was very sorry they could not clearly understand
me, so as to give them the order and plan of attacking their enemies, as we should indubitably defeat
them all; but there was no help for that; that I
was very glad to encourage them, and to manifest
to them my good will when we should be engaged.

"The moment we landed they began to run
about two hundred paces toward their enemies,
who stood firm, and had not yet perceived my
companions, who went into the bush with some
savages. Ours commenced calling me in a loud

voice, and making way for me, opened in two, and placed me at their head, marching about twenty paces in advance until I was within thirty paces of the enemy.

"The moment they saw me they halted, gazing at me and I at them. When I saw them preparing to shoot at us I raised my arquebus, and aiming directly at one of the three chiefs, two of them fell to the ground by this shot, and one of their companions received a wound, of which he died afterward. I had put four balls in my arquebus. Ours, in witnessing a shot so favorable to them, set up such tremendous shouts that thunder could not have been heard; and yet there was no lack of arrows on one side and the other. The Iroquois were greatly astonished, seeing two men killed so instantaneously, notwithstanding they were provided with arrow-proof armor woven of cotton thread and wood. This frightened them very much. Whilst I was reloading, one of my companions in the bush fired a shot which so astonished them anew, seeing their chiefs slain, that they lost courage, took to flight and abandoned the field and their fort, hiding themselves in the depths of the forest, whither pursuing them I killed some others. Our savages also killed several of them, and took ten or twelve prisoners. The rest carried off the wounded. Fifteen or six-

teen of ours were wounded by arrows; they were
promptly cured.

"After having gained the victory they amused
themselves plundering Indian corn and meal from
the enemy; also their arms, which they had thrown
down in order to run the better. And having
feasted, sung and danced, we returned, three hours
after, with the prisoners.

"The place where the battle was fought is 43
degrees some minutes latitude, and I named it
Lake Champlain."

It is probable that "the point of a cape which
puts into the lake on the west side," was Ticonderoga, and the place where the battle occurred the
flat just north of the old promontory, which is
situated about 43 degrees, 35 minutes, N. latitude.

CARILLON.

IESKAU moved from Fort St. Frederick in the summer of 1755 to fortify Ticonderoga, as a protection against Johnson's force, then marching toward Crown Point; but, hearing that he was then at the head of Lake George with the greater part of his force, leaving Fort Lyman (Edward) in a defenseless condition, the brave old baron, whose motto was "valor wins," decided to advance upon it at once. The result of the movement is detailed in the account of the battle of Lake George. At that time he commenced a fortification, which was completed the ensuing year, and called "CARILLON," meaning music, racket, a chime of bells, perhaps suggested by the perpetual chiming of the "sounding waters" near by.

The Indian name of Ticonderoga has been variously spelled, owing, probably, to the known difficulty of finding just the right letter to express a certain sound in a different tongue from our own. The word seems to mean the meeting of waters, rather than the explanation usually given of "sounding waters," which may have been the name of the falls above, but *not* of the old promontory, for the

Indians always gave names that meant something, and had some peculiar fitness to the thing named. *Tio-gen* meant " the junction of two waters;" *Deca-riaderoga* " the junction of lakes of two different qualities." In Pownell's map, published in London in 1774, it is marked *Cheonderoga*, and the explanation given is " three rivers." Colden, writing in 1765, says: " These names, though supposed to be proper names of places, are, really, common names in the Indian language, signifying a river or hill, or fall of water. Thus *Ticnderoga*, though to us the proper name of the fort between Lake George and Lake Champlain, signifies *the place where two rivers meet*, and many places are called by that name in the Indian language."

In 1757 Montcalm went out from the stronghold to the attack of Fort William, and returned victorious, but the leaves in his crown of laurel dripped with the blood of helpless women and children.

In 1758 General Abercrombie made his unsuccessful attack, and the following year Amherst entrenched before the old French lines, and prepared to lay seige to the fort. The French, finding that they could not hope to successfully resist, abandoned the works on the night of the twenty-sixth of July, setting fire to them as they went. The flames soon communicated with the shells and loaded guns, which kept up a continuous discharge

for some time ; then the English advanced and took
possession, finding no enemy to resist, save the fire,
which was soon extinguished. The French retreated down the lake, leaving Fort St. Frederick
also in possession of the English, who enlarged
and strengthened them on a scale of great magnifi-
cence, but never a shot or shell sped from the
costly embrasures against an advancing enemy;
while time passed, and, touching the massive walls,
they, piece by piece, fell away, and for want of an
object were never repaired, so that, when the
cloud which had so long threatened, burst, and the
colonies were at war with the mother country, they
scarcely afforded protection for the company of lazy
red coats composing the garison at the time.

ETHAN ALLEN.

HE question as to who originated the idea of capturing Ticonderoga has provoked much discussion, and it is not to be wondered at, if the same thought was suggested to the minds of several at the same time; but John Brown seems to have been the first to make a movement in that direction. He had passed through the New Hampshire settlements about the beginning of March, 1775, and wrote to Samuel Adams and Joseph Warren at Boston: "One thing I must mention, to be kept as a profound secret: The fort at Ticonderoga must be seized as soon as possible, should hostilities be committed by the king's troops; the people of the New Hampshire grants have engaged to do the business, and in my opinion they are the proper persons for the job."

The "Green Mountain Boys" were, without doubt, "the proper persons for the job." Ethan Allen's was the voice that called them together, and to him is due the credit of carrying the design to a successful termination, notwithstanding the views of quite a noted writer on the subject, who divides the honor between him and Benedict

4

Arnold, generously giving the latter the lion's share, as being the "duly commissioned" officer of the expedition. Arnold *was* duly commissioned by the Massachusetts committee of safety to raise men and proceed to take the fort in question, and he conceived the brilliant idea of raising a lot that were gathering around Ethan Allen at Castleton. So, hastening forward alone, he arrived as they were preparing to march, and applied for the command by virtue of his commission, which modest request was not granted. Even after this unjust treatment, with a generosity truly commendable, he was willing to allow Allen to accompany him as an equal, in consideration of the comparatively unimportant fact that the men would not go under any other commander. "By the judicious course of Arnold harmony was restored," and they proceeded on their way, having entered into an arrangement whereby they were to hold joint command — a sort of double-headed military monstrosity — one armed with *authority*, the other *power*.

To an American, Ethan Allen and Ticonderoga seem as one, and the history of the fort would be incomplete without that of the Green Mountain leader. He was born in 1738 in Connecticut, removing thence at an early age, and settling on the New Hampshire grants. A man of strong, natural endowments, energy and decision of character; an unyielding advocate of what he considered right. Beloved by friends and feared by foes he naturally became the leader of the settlers on the western slope, and took a prominent part in resisting the demands of New York, which State, claiming jurisdiction to the summit of the Green mountains, ejected settlers who did not receive a title from them, punished those who resisted, and declared Allen an outlaw, with a price set upon his head.

At the breaking out of the rebellion he raised a company of men and started to attack the fort, accompanied by Arnold, who was probably endured because of the commission which he held, while his presence made no difference in the movement of the men. From Allen's "Narrative," written in 1779, the following account of the capture is taken:

"Ever since I arrived at the state of manhood, and acquainted myself with the general history of mankind, I have felt a sincere passion for liberty. The history of nations, doomed to perpetual slavery, in consequence of yielding up to tyrants their natural-born liberties, I read with a sort of philosophical horror; so that the first systematical and bloody attempt at Lexington, to enslave America, thoroughly electrified my mind, and fully determined me to take part with my country. And, while I was wishing for an opportunity to signalize myself in its behalf, directions were privately sent to me

from the then colony (now State) of Connecticut, to
raise the Green Mountain Boys, and, if possible, to
surprise and take the fortress of Ticonderoga. This
enterprise I cheerfully undertook; and, after first
guarding all the several passes that led thither, to
cut off all intelligence between the garrison and the
country, made a forced march from Bennington,
and arrived at the lake opposite to Ticonderoga
on the evening of the ninth day of May, 1775, with
two hundred and thirty valiant Green Mountain
Boys; and it was with the utmost difficulty that I
procured boats to cross the lake. However, I
landed eighty-three men near the garrison, and sent
the boats back for the rear guard, commanded by
Col. Seth Warner; but the day began to dawn, and
I found myself under a necessity to attack the fort,
before the rear could cross the lake; and, as it was
viewed hazardous, I harangued the officers and
soldiers in the manner following:

"'Friends and fellow soldiers, you have, for a
number of years past been a scourge and terror
to arbitrary power. Your valor has been famed
abroad, and acknowledged, as appears by the ad-
vice and orders to me from the General Assembly
of Connecticut, to surprise and take the garrison
now before us. I now propose to advance before
you, and in person conduct you through the wicket-
gate; for we must this morning either quit our

pretensions to valor, or possess ourselves of this
fortress in a few minutes; and, inasmuch as it is a
desperate attempt, which none but the bravest of
men dare undertake, I do not urge it on any contrary to his will. You that will undertake volun-
tarily, poise your firelocks.'

"The men being, at this time, drawn up in three
ranks, each poised his firelock. I ordered them to
face to the right, and at the head of the center file,
marched them immediately to the wicket-gate
aforesaid, where I found a sentry posted, who
instantly snapped his fusee at me; I ran immediately toward him, and he retreated through the
covered way into the parade within the garrison,
gave a halloo, and run under a bomb-proof. My
party, who followed me into the fort, I formed on
the parade in such a manner as to face the two barracks which faced each other.

"The garrison being asleep, except the sentries,
we gave three huzzas, which greatly surprised
them. One of the sentries made a pass at one of
my officers with a charged bayonet, and slightly
wounded him. My first thought was to kill him
with my sword; but, in an instant I altered the
design and fury of the blow to a slight cut on the
side of the head; upon which he dropped his gun,
and asked quarter, which I readily granted him,
and demanded of him the place where the com-

manding officer kept; he shewed me a pair of stairs
in the front of a barrack, on the west part of the
garrison, which led up a second story in said barrack, to which I immediately repaired, and ordered
the commander, Capt. De La Place, to come forth
instantly, or I would sacrifice the whole garrison;
at which the captain came immediately to the door
with his breeches in his hand; when I ordered him
to deliver me the fort instantly; he asked me by
what authority I demanded it; I answered him,
‘ *In the name of the Great Jehovah, and the Conti-
nental Congress.*’   The authority of the Congress
being very little known at that time, he began to
speak again; but I interrupted him, and with my
drawn sword over his head, again demanded an
immediate surrender of the garrison; with which
he then complied, and ordered his men to be forth-
with paraded without arms, as he had given up
the garrison. In the mean time some of my officers
had given orders, and in consequence thereof, sun-
dry of the barrack doors were beat down, and
about one-third of the garrison imprisoned, which
consisted of the said commander, a Lieut. Feltham,
a conductor of artillery, a gunner, two sergeants,
and forty-four rank and file; about one hundred
pieces of cannon, one thirteen inch mortar, and a
number of swivels. This surprise was carried into
execution in the grey of the morning of the tenth

of May, 1775. The sun seemed to rise that morning with a superior lustre; and Ticonderoga and
its dependencies smiled on its conquerors, who
tossed about the flowing bowl, and wished success
to Congress, and the liberty and freedom of America. Happy it was for me, at that time, that the
then future pages of the book of fate, which afterward unfolded a miserable scene of two years and
eight months imprisonment, were hid from my view.

"But to return to my narration: Col. Warner,
with the rear guard, crossed the lake, and joined
me early in the morning, whom I sent off, without
loss of time, with about one hundred men, to take
possession of Crown Point, which was garrisoned
with a sergeant and twelve men, which he took
possession of the same day, as also upwards of one
hundred pieces of cannon."

In September of the same year Allen joined Maj.
John Brown in an expedition against Montreal,
was captured and sent to England, where the
populace looked upon the tall American as a great
curiosity; but the government found that they had
drawn an elephant, and did not know how to get
rid of him. He clearly deserved hanging, but,
unfortunately, the Yankees held too many loyal
Englishmen to make it safe to inaugurate such a
course of proceedings.

He was carried about to various places until January, 1777, when he was put aboard an English vessel, and spent most of the time until November sailing up and down the American seaboard, then allowed to go ashore on his parol. While awaiting in New York to be exchanged he was offered a colonel's commission and a large tract of land in either the New Hampshire grants or Connecticut if he would espouse the royal cause and help to subdue the rebels. His characteristic reply was:

"That, if by faithfulness I had recommended myself to Gen. Howe, I should be loth, by unfaithfulness, to lose the General's good opinion; besides, that I viewed the offer of land to be similar to that which the devil offered Jesus Christ, 'To give him all the kingdoms of the world, if he would fall down and worship him;' when, at the same time, the damned soul had not one foot of land upon earth."

In May, 1778, he was exchanged. He visited Washington at Valley Forge; was received by him with marks of approbation and esteem, and, after offering his further services in behalf of his country, returned to Bennington, where he arrived on the last day of May, with health much impaired by the trials he had undergone, and which, probably, hastened his death, which occurred February 13, 1789.

It is claimed by some that he was engaged in a treasonable movement, the object of which was to attach Vermont to Canada.   It is not reasonable to suppose that this man, who, in the darkest days of the rebellion, sick and in prison, refused wealth and a title, would have plotted treason to his country at a time when light was breaking, and the recollection of Bennington and Saratoga still fresh in the hearts of the people.   Rather let us consider it, what the result seemed to prove, a master stroke of diplomacy, which effectually stopped all military operations of the army under Haldiman, then at Ticonderoga, and for a long time protected the northern frontier from the depredations of the enemy.   Then came peace and rest to the soldier, who, had he been less a partizan, might have made fewer enemies, but not what he was, "*Ethan Allen*, the hero of Ticonderoga, the idol of the Green Mountain men."

1776 passed quietly at Ticonderoga, with the exception of an alarm caused by the approach of Sir Guy Carleton, who came as far south as Crown Point, and then withdrew into Canada again; but, with the summer of 1777, came, sweeping from the north, the brave, the accomplished, the conceited Burgoyne, bringing, in his train, 7,500 men, who prepared to attack Ticonderoga.   St. Clair, then in command, had barely sufficient troops to man the principal works, let alone the outposts. So, on the approach of the English, he abandoned his position outside, and retired within the old French lines. Burgoyne advanced and took possession; erected

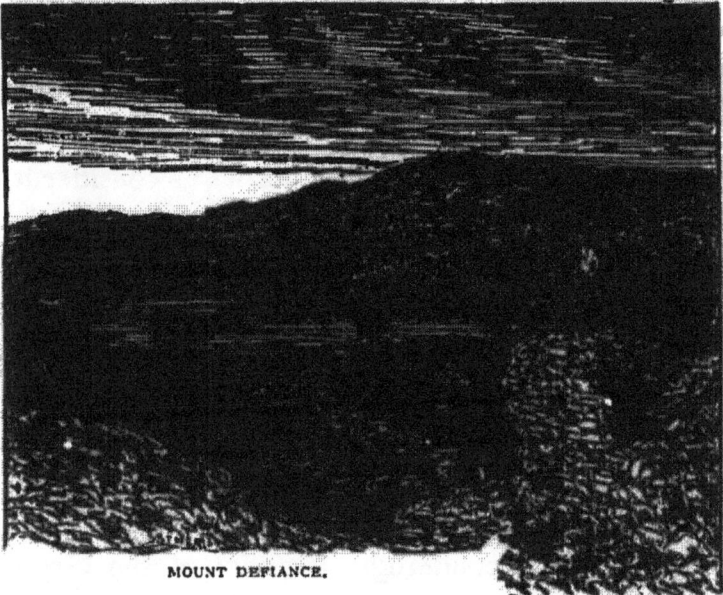

MOUNT DEFIANCE.

a battery on the rocky bluff, just north of where the village of Ticonderoga now stands, thereby cutting off all communication with Lake George, and, elated by the advantage gained, called it "Mount Hope." From this point a brisk cannonading was commenced, under cover of which a road was cut to the summit of Sugar Hill, and on the night of the 4th of July several cannon were conveyed to its summit, which they then named "Mount Defiance." When the morning of the 5th

broke, the garrison of St. Clair beheld, with astonishment and dismay, the guns of the English on
the top of the mountain, across the valley, scarcely
two miles distant, from which they could easily
throw shot and shell right down into the midst of
the fortification. A council of war was called, and
an evacuation decided upon; but, as every movement within the fort could be distinctly seen from
Mount Defiance, the men were not told of the
decision of the commandant until after dark.
"Then there was hurrying to and fro;" all that
could be removed was taken. Guns that could not
be taken were spiked; and shortly after midnight
the stars looked down on a throng moving silently
away across the chain-bridge. Then, once more, ·
the grim old fortress was left silent and alone.

Contrary to express orders, one of the soldiers,
on abandoning Mount Independence, set fire to a
house, and the light streaming far out, across the
water, revealed the retreating Americans to the
watchful foe. They hastened their flight, and the
greater part, taking the road toward Castleton,
were followed and engaged by the English, who
complained that "*the Green Mountain Boys took
sight.*" The result was a victory for the English,
with a loss of nearly ten to one of the Yankees.

The others, retreating up Wood creek to Skeens-
boro', were pursued by Burgoyne, who broke

through the chain bridge and reached the landing
nearly as soon as they, capturing most of the
stores and ammunition, the men escaping to Fort
Ann.

St. Clair was removed from his command, but
at an after-investigation justified and honored for
the moral bravery displayed in choosing to sacrifice his own reputation rather than the lives of his
soldiers.   Then came the story of

> "The Green Mountaineer — the Stark of Bennington,
>   When on that field his band the Hessians fought,
> Briefly he spoke before the fight began :
>   'Soldiers! those German gentlemen are bought
> For four pounds eight and seven pence per man,
>   By England's king ; a bargain as is thought.
> Are we worth more ?   Let's prove it now we can ;
>   For we must beat them, boys, ere set of sun,
> OR MOLLIE STARK'S A WIDOW.'   *It was done.*"

Then " Saratoga," bringing humiliation to the
English and joy to the struggling patriots, and the
garrison at Ticonderoga dismantling the old fort,
retired into Canada.

It was occupied again in 1780 by the forces
under General Haldiman, and was the scene of
those bloodless battles of diplomacy where Allen
plotted treason with such consummate sagacity
that his bitterest enemy could find nothing to jus-
tify their suspicions of wrong; all of which goes
to prove him a very subtle villain indeed.   Meanwhile the enemy of his country rested on their

arms along the northern frontier, " and peace reigned throughout her borders."

Then once again an enemy attacked the old fort. Coming not with the sound of martial music and the gay trappings of the soldiery, but with banners of trailing cloud and drifting mist, with music of wind and rain and echoing thunder, while frosts rack and tempests beat upon the frowning walls, which crumble and fall away, and nature, reclaiming her own, tenderly covers it over with springing grass and creeping vines, hastening the time when nothing shall remain to tell the story of the past but the sounding name that the Red Men gave it long ago.

5

HE Fort Ticonderoga Hotel was built in 1826 by William F. Pell for a summer residence, and first occupied as a hotel in 1840, when the grounds were thrown open to the public.

The central portion is two stories high; the front sustained by massive columns, around which vines cling and climb to the very top. On each side extends long, low wings, with suits of rooms at the extreme ends, which can be entered from the outside or through the glass-enclosed verandah from the main building. The hotel fac he east, is fronted by a tree-covered lawn, through which a plank walk leads down to the steamboat dock, and a road runs through the fields to the depot a little to the north, over which a free carriage conveys guests to and from all trains. The house is open day and night; the principal business is the dinners, which are first-class, and partaken of by hungry travelers while waiting for the boats; and, altogether, it is a very enjoyable place, unless it rains, in which case (to use a strong word, and one with a smack of profanity about it, perfectly plain to those who have been thereabouts at such times) it is simply " Ticonderoga."

MAP OF THE RUINS

IN

1873,

ACCOMPANYING STODDARD'S

"TICONDEROGA."

—o—

1. Parade Ground.
2. North Bastion.
3. West Bastion.
4. South Barracks.
5. East Barracks.
6. West Barracks; officers' quarters.
7. Underground room.
8. Underground room; fallen in.
9. Underground room; fallen in.
10. Entrance and sally-port.
11. Path leading into the fort.
12. Covered way, place where
   Allen entered.
13. Moat.
14. Line of breastworks.
15. Glacis—open field.
16. Entrance to underground room.
17. Bomb-proof.
18. To the old French lines.
19. To the Grenadier Battery.
20. To Mount Defiance.
21. To the old fort well and hotel.
22. Entrance to Parade Ground.

THE BARRACKS.

PRESENT STATE OF THE RUINS.

ROM the south end of the hotel a path leads across the field, where, at its outskirts, we climb over the stone wall, and, following along under the locusts, a little way to the south come to the " old fort well," a never failing spring, the green, slimy home of the frog and the lizard, nearly filled with stones and clinging alders. Crossing the road we follow along up the stone fence over the very road pursued by Allen on that May morning nearly a century ago. There is little doubt about it.

Allen's narrative, the various traditions, and the testimony of Isaac Rice, whose brother was with Allen at the time, establish this fact, as well as that of the place where the commandant slept, and where he stood when the tall Vermonter demanded the surrender. The old soldier, who, himself, performed garrison duty, under St. Clair, for many years acted as a guide at the ruins, and was buried, at his own request, within the fortress,* there to sleep until the great reveille shall sound, and he rises to answer at roll-call, in a world that has no ruins.

A great pile of stones mark the spot where once existed the entrance to the covered way (*protected way* would be better understood among unmilitary people, as it protected a person within it from an enemy at the sides only, being open at the top), where the sentry snapped his fusee at Allen. The walls are thirty-three inches apart, and can be easily traced to where they seem to enter the fort at the south-east corner of the parade-ground. The walls of the barrack, on the west, where the commandant slept, are still standing ; those on the south are nearly gone, while the cellar only shows where the east line stood. Along the north side is what was probably the bomb-proof, under which the soldier ran when pursued by Allen. The foundation can be traced along the front and across the ends. On the side toward the parade are the remains of four heavy piers or columns of mason work, which supported the roof. Under this men could retire, and, through the embrasures that

* Cook.

looked out toward the north, bring guns to bear on
an enemy approaching from that direction.

I am aware that this statement is not in accord-
ance with any other given; but I consider the
proof sufficient to carry me out in the assertion.
The outline of all the walls are perfectly plain.
The foundation of this one is well preserved; the
corners sharp, and unmistakably *made so*, as well as
the piers built on the inside for the (probable) sup-
port of the roof. If this ever had a fourth wall,
why should all trace of it be wanting at the present
day, when others are so plainly defined? The fact
that the retreating soldier ran into the parade first
is presumptive evidence that he had to do so to
reach the bomb-proof. Allen says: "My party,
who followed me into the fort, I formed, on the
parade, in such a manner as to face the two barracks, *which face each other*." It is evident that
Allen meant, by that sentence, to describe the
position that his men occupied; but if the barracks
faced each other on the north and south, as well as
on the east and west, the sentence would be mere
foolishness, and express nothing. The idea that
there were barracks on the four sides, probably,
grew out of the fact that there were four buildings,
but two of the four were on the south side, and
between them the main entrance to the parade.

Let us go to the place where Allen entered, at the south end of the east line of barracks, which is here cut off on a line with the parade by a descending alley, looking out toward the old well, and continued in the trench and double line of walls which was the covered way. We wonder at the peculiar shape of the foundation on the extreme point of this corner, like in shape to the head of an Indian arrow, the point extending outward. Half way down to the point of the promontory a rocky ledge crops out. Extending beyond is the remains of an old battery or covered way. On the brow of the promontory, commanding the lake for quite a distance, as it circles around, is the grenadier battery, a substantial looking, stone and earth fort, designed for heavy guns, having seven angles, the side fronting the water curved inward. It is said to have been the one commenced by Baron Dieskau in 1755. The chain or floating bridge extended from near the steamboat landing to the point on the opposite shore where you will find, near the foot of the hill, the water battery, and, higher up, lines of breastworks; while on the summit is the ruins of what, in '76, was a picket fort, surrounding a square of barracks. Here are the graves of many soldiers, their last resting place marked by little, rough headstones—"nameless, all but one, and that a name unknown."

Returning to the old fort, we find at the south-west corner, just outside of the barracks, the surface broken and thrown up into grassy mounds,

THE BARRACK WINDOW.

marking the position of one of the three underground rooms which existed at the time Amherst took possession of the fort; the second is found in a similar condition to the first, at the north-west corner; the door and entrance from the cellar of the officers' quarters being quite well preserved now. Following along the hollow that seems to mark the course of an underground passage to the north-east corner, you stand over the third, which is one of the best preserved portions of the ruins. To enter you climb down into the cellar, now nearly filled with broken stones and overrun with vines, and, stooping low, make your way through the opening before you.

At one time a man could enter erect, but now stones stop the way, and earth and stones half fill the room beneath. You find it is bomb-proof, about twelve feet wide by thirty long, with arched roof; the entrance at the south-west corner; at the south is a large sky-light; at the east end a small, chimney-like aperture; at each corner of this end are small circular rooms, with arched roof, one about seven, the other ten, feet in diameter. At the west end the side wall has fallen in, where, apparently, an underground passage led off toward the room at the west barrack, the indication of which can be traced along the surface. What this was for is a matter of supposition. Some say that this was the bakery, and it is generally

spoken of as such. But was it necessary to have
the bakery so well protected? Military men generally say that it was the magazine. "You pays
your money and you takes your choice."

Come out and stand once more on the rounded
top. At our feet is a deep ditch; in the center, on
the north and west, are two high bastions commanding the approach from these directions;
around them also flows the trench in which troops
could be marched and massed at any desired point
within the circuit. Outside of the ditch, following
its various angles, is the outer wall, once breast
high, but now almost level with the plain, and the
glacis slopes off toward Champlain on the north,
and upward toward the old French lines at the
north-west.

Turning toward the sunrise we look down over
the old camp well, the waving locusts and grove,
where stands the hotel with its double guard of
spectral looking poplars, and the field to the north,
which is probably the scene of Champlain's battle
with the Iroquois over two hundred years ago.

A long bridge stretches away across the lake,
and a huge, white, floating draw swings open and
shut as the steamers come and go. Just a little
north, on the further shore, is the place where, on
the evening of the 9th of May, 1775, the Green
Mountain Boys gathered, with eyes set toward the

old fort; while away beyond, where the mountains slope toward the west, from their blue summit to the water's edge, lies the disputed territory — the New Hampshire grants.

Turn back a hundred pages in the book of time. It is night — one of those bright, dewy ones that heralds the approach of a day of uncommon loveliness. Knowing all things, we understand the thoughts of those who gather on that further shore, and as the stars, slowly rising above the eastern mountains, proclaim the coming morn, we see the dusky throng come up out of the water, and stand silently on this side. Now a tall form steps out from among the little band; we hear the brief harangue, and see every gun poised in token of their willingness to follow where ETHAN ALLEN leads. We follow their stealthy march across the lowland, past the old fort well, and up the path to the wicket-gate. The startled sentry raises his gun at the leader, but no sound follows the motion. Perhaps it was not loaded; the lazy red coats were not expecting an enemy so soon. Now the attacking party follow the retreating soldier through the covered way into the parade, and hastily form in two lines, facing the barracks, which face each other, not ruins now, but grim and stately they stand — east, west and south — with a balcony on a line with the second floor, across the front of each.

The gray of the May morning is turning into crimson, and the chimney tops are penciled with gold, as the loud huzzas of the Green Mountain men wake the echoes of the old fortress. A sentry makes a pass at one of Allen's officers. Like a gleam of light the sword of the leader describes a circle in the air, and descends on the head of the rash man; but the fierce flash of anger that gave fury to the blow is tempered with mercy, and turns it aside in its descent. The musket falls to the ground, and the frightened soldier begs for life, which Allen grants, demanding to be shown where the commandant sleeps. He is directed to a stairway that leads up to the gallery of the west line of barracks, and up this he goes, while the sound of crashing doors break on the ears of the half-awakened garrison. When near the south end of the building he thumps loudly on a door with the hilt of his heavy sword. Captain De La Place appears with astonishment on his face, and his small clothes in his hands, while his young wife stands tremblingly behind him. He has no time to parley, for the giant form of the Yankee leader towers up before him, demanding the surrender by authority higher than he had ever dreamed; he hasn't even time to find out whether Allen is duly commissioned or not. A man is never wholly a man with his boots off; so what *can* a poor little

British officer, with only one garment on, do, but surrender when that great sword is suspended threateningly above his head. The order is given, the garrison parades without arms, and the rising sun shines on the first English prisoner of the revolution.

But where is that gold-laced, duly commissioned brain which contributed so much to the success of the enterprize, "without whom the expedition possibly might have failed?" If Arnold entered first, as he claims, why did the sentry at the wicket gate pay that delicate little attention to Allen instead of him? Bancroft says of Allen : "Placing himself at the head of the center file, Arnold keeping emulously at his side, he marched to the gate."

In a late work on Lake George the author quotes a part of the above, but in such a manner that the reader is left in doubt, while he rather inclines to the opinion that Allen is the emulous individual referred to.

Imagine for a moment the stupendous Benedict sweeping majestically onward, with the little Vermonter trotting emulously along at his side. Arnold claims, in his report to the committee on safety, that he was "the first who entered and took possession of the fort;" probably in the same manner that he took command of the men at Castleton,

6

concerning which Bancroft says, when Arnold
claimed command by virtue of the commission
given him by this same committee, it " was disre-
garded, and the men unanimously elected Ethan
Allen their chief."

"Arnold's bravery was never questioned."
Neither was his assurance; but the position that
he occupied on this occasion seems to have been
that of a sort of ornamental figure-head — a military necessity, in shape of a magnificently gotten
up uniform, which would have answered every
purpose if the occupant had been dropped out
somewhere on the road and lost.

But, to return once more to the ruins of to-day.
We cross the parade, which is about fifty paces
long, and twenty-two broad, to the south-west
corner; pass through the alley, out over the fallen
bomb-proof room, down into the ditch, and, crossing at the left of the west bastion, go up the
inclined plane (which was the entrance and sally-
port), toward the north, noticing that the walls lap,
one past the other, like those of a snail-shell, the
inleading path circling around until it enters the
parade on the south. Beside the natural defenses
on this unexposed side a narrow wall was considered sufficient protection. Toward the west the
surface of the promontory breaks suddenly away,
descending nearly a hundred feet in its slope to the

water's edge. That ditch, in which stands the great, wavy elm, is said to have been a covered way to the lake. Alders and thorn-trees grow on the hillside; the red-plumed sumachs press up the steep, and clinging ivy, mounting upward, where an enemy could not hope to climb, covers the gray rocks with a robe of living green. Across the valley is Mount Defiance, sloping gently to the north, up which, on that anniversary prospective, many years ago, Burgoyne's men went, dragging the heavy cannon which greeted St. Clair, as he looked toward its summit, the morning after.

Of the many traditions that cluster around the place we will repeat but one—found in Cook's "Ticonderoga," and apparently well authenticated: An Indian girl, of remarkable beauty, was confined in this fortress by one of the French officers. Frightened by his coarse attention, her life became a continual torture, and escape at any price was preferable to remaining there in his power. Walking, by compulsion, with him one night upon the western wall, preferring death to dishonor, she sprang away, over the giddy parapet, meeting her death upon the rocks below, but with the wild spirit, as it left the mangled, bleeding form, went up a savage cry for vengeance, that descended, swift and sure on the head of him who had driven her across the dark river.

Seated here, on the western wall, of a summer afternoon the mind is entranced, and the spirit held captive, by the exquisite beauty of the scene. What harmonious combinations of strength and delicacy in the brilliant, rocky foreground, and dreamy, tender distance; what sparkling bits of light, of broad, sweet shadow, down in the depths of that radiant sea of haze, out of which gleams glittering gems, and bits of fallen sky. The sun, sinking behind the wooded summit of Mount Defiance, pencils long lines of gold through an atmosphere of misty white, tipping the tree tops with light, while the hillside, sloping toward us, is resting all in cool, gray shadow. The river comes winding down through reedy flats, and patches of bright and sombre green, under the long bridge, stretching away across to the south, past the belt of graceful elms and clumps of alders that fringe the meadow, over which a flock of sheep are wending their slow way homeward, nipping, here and there, a tender bit of grass as they go.

The trees cast long shadows across the meadow, lengthening out toward us, until overtaken and absorbed by that of the mountain. Slowly the last crimson ray retreats before the advancing shadows; slowly it climbs the steep hillside, glorifying the rocks, shining among the thorn-apples, lingering in the masses of dark green, outlining their shadowy forms, with edges of light, rests lovingly upon the sumacs, whose brilliant plumes glow with an added fire, then burning a moment on the grey wall, die out, while the shining bars rise up higher and higher, and streaming away out over our heads across the valley to the east, kiss the summits of the distant mountains good night, and mount upward into the world of light from whence they came.

As the shadows of night come down over us, the twitter of little birds settling to rest is heard ; the circling night hawk, with his lonesome cry, comes sweeping past ; the voice of the whippoor-will is in the thicket; the cricket chirps among the stones; the sound of waves plashing on the beach is borne faintly on the odor-laden air ; a monoto-nous song comes up from the swamp, and the myriad voices of a summer night all blend together in inexpressible harmony, while one by one the eternal stars come out and look pityingly down on the dim old walls and darkling battlements of Ticonderoga.

CHAMPLAIN STEAMERS.

"VERMONT," · ·	Captain	**WILLIAM H. FLAGG**
"ADIRONDACK," · ·	"	**WM. ANDERSON**
"UNITED STATES," · ·	"	**GEO. RUSHLOW.**
"OAKES AMES," (Ferry) ·	"	**B. J. HOLT.**

SUMMER ARRANGEMENT, 1873.

DAY BOAT.

		NORTH.	SOUTH.
Monday,	- -	ADIRONDACK.	VERMONT.
Tuesday,	- -	UNITED STATES.	ADIRONDACK.
Wednesday,	- -	VERMONT.	ADIRONDACK.
Thursday,	- -	UNITED STATES.	VERMONT.
Friday,	- -	ADIRONDACK.	VERMONT.
Saturday,	- -	UNITED STATES.	ADIRONDACK.

NIGHT BOAT.

		NORTH.	SOUTH.
Monday,	· · ·	VERMONT.	UNITED STATES.
Tuesday,	· · ·	ADIRONDACK.	VERMONT.
Wednesday,	· · ·	ADIRONDACK.	UNITED STATES.
Thursday,	· · ·	VERMONT.	ADIRONDACK.
Friday,	· · ·	VERMONT.	UNITED STATES.
Saturday,	· · ·	None.	None.

CONNECTIONS.

WHITEHALL,—R. and S. R. R. **TICONDEROGA,**—Stages, and Steamers through Lake George. **BURLINGTON,**—Vt. Central R. R. **PORT KENT,**—Stages for Keeseville and the Adirondacks. **PLATTSBURGH,** —N. Y. and Canada R. R. **ROUSE'S POINT,**—O. & L. C. and Grand Trunk Railroads.

DAY BOAT—(GOING SOUTH)—Leaves Rouse's Point on the arrival of train from Montreal and Ogdensburg, 8.15 A. M., breakfast on board; Plattsburgh, (ferry) 8.00 A. M.; Port Kent, 8.45 A. M.; arrive at Burlington, 10.45 A. M.; Ticonderoga, 2.30 P. M.; Whitehall, 4.45; Saratoga, (via R. R.) 6.35; Albany, 8.30 P. M.; New York, 6.00 A. M.

NIGHT BOAT—(GOING SOUTH)—Leaves Rouse's Point on the arrival of trains from Montreal and Ogdensburg 5.40 P. M., supper on board; Plattsburgh, 7.45 P. M.; Port Kent, 8.45 P. M.; arrive at Burlington, 9.30 P. M.; Ticonderoga, 2.30 A. M.; Whitehall, 5.45 A. M.; Saratoga, (via R.R.) 7.45 A. M.; Albany, 9.45 A. M.; New York, 2.30 P. M.

DAY BOAT—(GOING NORTH)—Leaves Whitehall on arrival of trains from New York, Troy, Albany and Saratoga, 10.45 A. M., dine on board, and arrive at Ticonderoga, 12.45; Burlington, 5.00; Port Kent, 5.40; Plattsburgh 7 00 Rouse's Point, 9.00; St. Johns, (via R. R.) 10.00; Montreal, 11.00 P M

NIGHT BOAT—(GOING NORTH)—Leaves Whitehall on arrival of trains from New York, Troy, Albany and Saratoga, 8.20 P. M.; supper on board, and arrive at Ticonderoga, 10.15 P. M.; Burlington, 3.00 A. M.; Port Kent, 3.40; Plattsburgh, 5.00; Rouse's Point, 7.00; St. Johns, (via R. R.) 8.30; Montreal, 10.00; Malone, 10.07; Potsdam, 11.35 A. M.; Ogdensburg, 12.35 P. M.

TABLE OF CONTENTS.

68   CONTENTS.

—

www.ingramcontent.com/pod-product-compliance
Lightning Source LLC
Chambersburg PA
CBHW021514090426
42739CB00007B/612